*Celebration of Latinos in Loyola
University Chicago circa 2014*

ABOLISH RED LIGHT CAMS
BAN RED LIGHT & SPEED CAMERAS
www.banthe
Rahm Give The Money Back!!!
ABOLISH RED LIGHT CAMS
GOT TICKETS? BLAME SOLIS
JOIN THE FIGHT
ABOLISH RED LIGHT CAMS
GOT TICKETS? BLAME SUAREZ

TABLE OF CONTENTS

Youth

Ah, to be young again

And to enjoy one's youth is priceless

We can never go back in time

But only reminisce on our precious childhood memories

Memorable ones that make us laugh and contemplate on the good old days

Days where laughter and fun

Were in abundance

My favorite past time

Was going to the playground

And playing on the monkey bars

Swinging side to side

Swinging forwards

Hanging off them like

Silly little monkeys

Competing with your friends

With cool monkey bar tricks

Ah, yes to be young again.

LIFE

We've been through all of this before

Birth

Birthdays

Celebrations

Disappointments

Happiness

Good times

Bad times

Sadness

Dark times

Times to think

Time to see

Time to hear

Time to listen

Times to be silent

Times to reinvent Yourself

Times to Reflect

That's Life!

Lajas

Walking by the shores

And gazing at the crystallized waters

Seeing the sea life swim about

The beautiful Sea.

Mesmerized by the sheer

Beauty of Nature

The Peace and Tranquility

Waiting patiently to board a boat

And experience the Bioluminescent Bay

For the first time.

The engines rev up and we drive out

For miles into the pure darkness

Unable to see each other

We all gaze at the stars

And in unison we all say,

"You don't get to see this every day."

We're all in awe

The stars watching us back

Diligently gazing at us-

Millions of them.

Then it finally happens

We get to experience

One of the greatest wonders of the world

We see the live sea life

In the waters

We caress the sea with

Our bodies embracing the

Light that glows magically

Around our flesh

Around my skin

In the Bioluminescent Bay in

Lajas, Puerto Rico.

What is beauty

What is Beauty

Who defines Beauty

Why is there so much commotion

Towards the concept of Beauty

Why does Beauty have to come with a cost

Can't we just decide without

The propaganda that defines Beauty without the

Consent of Beauty itself

We decide what Beauty is

We decide who is Beautiful

We decide what experiences

Bring about Beauty in each other

And in Nature.

Once again what is Beauty?

Mamá

My Taino roots run deep

With the Love of my Grandmother

And my Great Great Grandmother

Who meditated Indian style

Who wore two black braids

Who believed in our deep

Rooted traditions of our

Indigenous Caribbean

Ancestry

West African blood

Taino blood

Spanish blood

Caribbean blood

Being Caribbean with the

Kiss of the Sun on our flesh

Our Taino sun surrounding

Our Caribbean waters and the Sea

The warmth of the Sun

The warmth of my Taino heritage

The warmth of my Grandmother, MAMÁ!

ROOTS

I have direct lineage to Rosa Parks

I have direct lineage to Malcolm X

I have direct lineage to Geraldo from the Young
Lords

I have direct lineage to the Black Panthers

I have direct lineage to Rosie Perez

How you may ask?

By the Fire that we all have

Inside of us to fight for Justice

By the Fire that we all have

Inside of us to fight against racism

By the Fire that we all have

Inside of us to oust racist pricks,

racist entities and systemic issues

that are over a thousand years old

I stand before you as a Afro Latina

That isn't scared of exposing

The ugliness of racism,

Exposing the ugliness of racist individuals,

And exposing those that always try to keep the

Black Man, Black Woman, Indigenous Man,

Indigenous Woman, Latina, Latino,

People of Color trampled

Under the feet of their

White Saviorness

I don't need a White Savior

I never have and never will

So keep your fakeness to yourself

Keep your flattering words to yourself

I can see you from 100 miles away

I have always seen you since I was a child

You forced me to learn English

You forced me to assimilate

You forced me to see the wrong in my Puerto
Ricanness,

But there is nothing wrong with my Puerto
Ricanness.

There is nothing wrong with my Culture

There is nothing wrong with my Ethnicity

There is nothing wrong in being Multi-Cultural

and Multi-Ethnic.

There is nothing wrong with being Afro Latina!

The Train

The train the train

It's always the same

With people going to work mindlessly

With people going to school

With people loitering

With children with adult supervision

With children alone unattended

The train the train

With smells of Weed

With people smoking cigarettes

The Blue Line the Green Line

My Trains My Trains

Twenty three years on

My Trains My Trains

You never cease to disappoint me

You are always the same

The train the train

My Trains My Trains

I am

I am she

I am who you are looking for

I am Afro Latina with ancestral roots

From West Africa

Spain, France, and from the

Tainos.

My people were enslaved

and mistreated

My people were raped and

tossed to the side.

My people faced genocide

My people faced monstrosities

by the New World and by the

Old World.

My lineage has seen great bloodshed

My lineage still sees discrimination

My lineage still endures mistreatments

My lineage is Strong

My lineage is Tenacious

My lineage will Never Back Down

My lineage is of Great Warriors

I am Taina

I am Africa

I am Afro Latina

I am!

<u>Soy Puertorriqueña</u>

Soy Puertorriqueña de la Isla

Soy Puertorriqueña de la Cepa

Del palo de Mangó

Besito de coco

Que le encanta avena de coco

Soy Puertorriqueña con raices
Fuerte
Soy Puertorriqueña con raices
Indigenas de los Tainos

Soy Puertorriqueña

Soy Taina

Soy Africana

Soy Afro Latina

   ¡Soy!

This specific book was written by the beauty I always experience in my motherland of Puerto Rico. In Puerto Rico my body, soul, and mind are aligned. My soul is engulfed by Peace and Happiness each time I visit Puerto Rico. If it were up to me I would just live on the island, but I have been called to live in Chicago. I have been able to help thousands here with my activism and community development that has played a crucial part in my other home - Chicago. I along with a collective from Hermosa Neighborhood Association with both Colin Bird and Neighbor Space was able to have the first Community Garden built in Hermosa/Belmont Cragin off of Diversey and Kilpatrick-it's original name was "Nuestra Hermosa" but others changed it to Belmont Cragin Community Garden. This was a $400,000.00 project. I was the chair of the Borinqueneer Mural an $80,000.00 project that is under the Metra Healy Station off of Fullerton and Pulaski. I lobbied for my school Foreman College and Career Academy to receive $1.8 million in Tifs. I helped Northwest Middle School earn a school improvement grant of $350,000.00. Did I receive any compensation for any of the above community development? NO!!!

That's not the purpose of my activism.
It is to allow others to see that there
is still good in the world. It's about
letting your light shine in a world of
darkness. I just hope to inspire and
create other change agents like myself
that will eventually become Social
Justice Practitioners.

Much love and respect to all of my
people in Chicago.

Besitos,

Irma Iris